# Infinity Pools

# Infinity Pools

Ana G. Cañizares

**COLLINS | DESIGN**

*An Imprint of* HarperCollins*Publishers*

INFINITY POOLS
Copyright © 2006 COLLINS DESIGN and LOFT Publications

HarperCollins books may be purchased for educational, business, or sales promotional use.
For information, please write: Special Markets Department, HarperCollins Publishers Inc.,
10 East 53rd Street, New York, NY 10022

First Edition published in 2006 by:
Collins Design
*An Imprint of* HarperCollins*Publishers*
10 East 53rd Street
New York, NY 10022
Tel.: (212) 207-7000
Fax: (212) 207-7654
collinsdesign@harpercollins.com
www.harpercollins.com

Distributed throughout the world by:
HarperCollins*Publishers*
10 East 53rd Street
New York, NY 10022
Fax: (212) 207-7654

Packaged by
LOFT Publications
Via Laietana, 32 4.° Of. 92
08003 Barcelona, Spain
Tel.: +34 932 688 088
Fax: +34 932 687 073
loft@loftpublications.com
www.loftpublications.com

Editor:
Ana G. Cañizares

Art Director:
Mireia Casanovas Soley

Layout:
Jonathan Roura Ponce

Library of Congress Cataloging-in-Publication Data

Cañizares, Ana Cristina G.
 Infinity pools / Ana G. Cañizares.--1st ed.
     p. cm.
  ISBN-13: 978-0-06-089340-8 (hardcover)
  ISBN-10: 0-06-089340-0 (hardcover)
 1. Swimming Pools. I. Title
 TH4763 .C36 2006
 728'.962--dc23

Printed in Spain
First Printing, 2006

# Contents

# Introduction

Known to have been first built by the Greeks and Romans for athletic training and nautical games, swimming pools were introduced into the private space by Roman emperors who incorporated fish into their private pools, hence the Latin word for fishpond, piscina. The swimming pool has come a long way since then, serving not only as a practical means of cooling off and exercising at home, but also as a luxurious architectural element capable of transforming atmospheres, creating fresh perspectives, and adding a new dimension to any household. The evolution of pool design has seen the emergence of distinct trends over the years, ranging from more elaborate compositions to rustic styles and organic forms, and finally to austere, minimalist structures and cutting-edge designs.

Undoubtedly, one of the most popular designs today, as well as one of the most expensive, is the infinity edge-pool, preferred by top landscape architects and design experts in the field. The term infinity derives from the visual effect produced by one or more edges of a pool being submerged below water level so that the water surface merges with the horizon, providing the illusion of an infinite plane. This effect is particularly impressive when the invisible edge is set against a larger body of water such as the ocean, or perched on an elevated site so that the sky becomes the backdrop. The illusion of continuity and stunning visual effects produced by this design are what make it perhaps the most coveted kind of swimming pool on the market.

Needless to say, building a private pool entails considerable costs and the hiring of skilled professionals, especially in the case of infinity pools because of the complexity of their high-tech design. In order for the water to spill over the edge, a dedicated system is required to collect the overflow in a trough and pump it back into the pool. The site-whether atop a cliff, along a hillside, or on flat terrain-also determines the extent of the project and the way in which the pool is designed so as to achieve the most striking visual effect possible. Pools that are built on flat land, for example, are often raised off the ground to create a perspective of continuity between the pool water and the landscape beyond, as would naturally occur with a pool already situated at a high altitude or on a sloping site. Although the classical rectangular shape is probably the most popular today for this kind of design, infinity pools can take any shape or form within the restrictions of the site. Other designs include lap pools, conceived for swimmers and characterized by their long and narrow shape; play pools, which are relatively smaller in size and appropriate for children; free-form pools, notable for their organic features and the integration of natural elements such as plants and stones; and asymmetric pools, which adhere to a linear scheme that uniquely adapts to the qualities of the site. A variety of accessories can be applied to enhance both the aspect and the function of a pool; this includes anything from fountains, boulders, and underwater seats to a pool entry that simulates a beach, fiber-optic lights, and automated heating, lighting, and sound systems.

Unlike decorating a home, where choices in furniture and accessories are easily modified or replaced, a swimming pool is literally cast in concrete, and revamping it can be costly and time-consuming. Evaluating the characteristics of the site, its climatic conditions, and the possible obstacles before construction begins is crucial to obtaining the desired result in the shortest amount of time. Keeping this in mind, experts say that it can take up to six months to build a high-end pool, assuming that the best masons and materials are available immediately.

Swimming pools have become a significant architectural element in residential landscape design and contemporary pools are created as much for esthetic reasons as practical ones. Designing the perfect pool for your needs requires balancing your artistic preferences with the expected uses of the pool and the possibilities or limitations imposed by the site. *Infinity Pools* showcases an array of stunning projects from around the world, situated in breathtaking locations and designed by international architects, illustrating the diversity of styles and concepts in today's pool designs and providing inspiration to homeowners and professionals alike.

Photos © Douglas Hill Photography, Barry Beer Design

## Pool in Malibu

Location: Malibu, CA, USA

Architect: Barry Beer Design

Conceived as the focal point of a private residence located along the California coastline, this infinity pool manages to improve the already stunning vistas from atop the 75-foot oceanfront cliff on which it is situated. Aiming to blur the distinction between architecture and nature, the architect fulfilled the owner's wish to have an exercise pool and spa that would create a dramatic effect and become the visual highlight of this waterfront home.

The pool can be seen from a central glass corridor through which you enter the house, immediately provoking a strong visual response that attracts attention to the beautiful views of the Pacific Ocean. A long, gentle curve pulls water to the edge of the pool, where it spills over a concealed wall to form a continuous plane of water that merges with the ocean and horizon. The imperceptible transition between pool and ocean was further emphasized by the use of gray plaster and a slate spillway edge, which matches almost to perfection the color of the ocean.

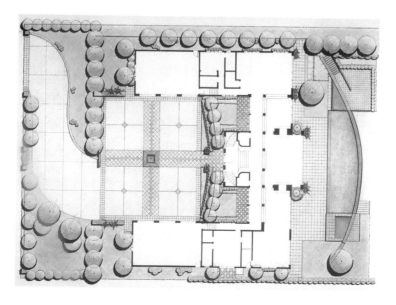

Plan

By choosing colors and materials that match the beach setting
in which this residence is located, the pool
blends seamlessly into the landscape.

# House Ray 1

Location: Vienna, Austria

Architect: Delugan Meissl Associated Architects

Situated on the flat roof of a 1960s office building in Vienna's fourth district, this apartment incorporates an infinity pool that looks out over the city's rooftop landscape. The residents were faced with strict building regulations, which they resolved by creating a homogeneous steel framework distributed over staggered levels that respects the adjacent buildings and provides a dynamic relationship between interior and exterior.

The recesses and folds of the new extension provide the opportunity to experience the structure's open layout from the entrance all the way up to the accessible roof area. Conceived as a sunken balustrade, the water basin at the edge of the roof was introduced to produce a dramatic effect and evoke in the spectator a sensation of continuity and the abyss. The pool steps function as seats from which to enjoy the rooftop views during the warmer months, while having the water level flush with the floor level cre-ates a smooth interface between the terrace and the urban landscape.

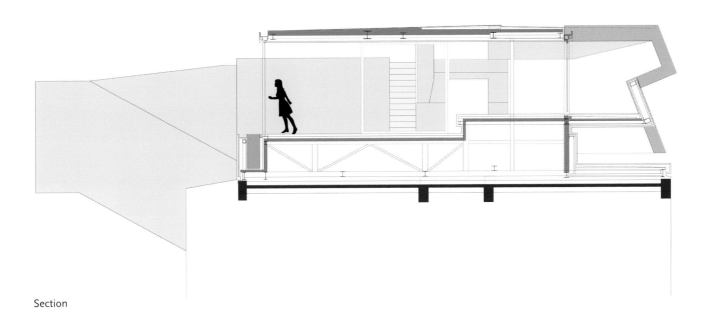

Section

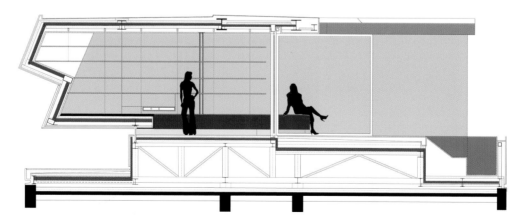

Section

Photos © Jordi Miralles

## Ocotal Beach

Location: Playa Ocotal, Costa Rica

Architect: Juan Roca Vallejo and Victor Cañas

This contemporary house sits on a mountainside not more than 650 feet from the shore of the Pacific Ocean. The owner, an architect himself, wished to make the minimalist house look as if it were floating on water, and he worked in conjunction with Juan Roca Vallejo on the design.

In order to achieve this effect, a shallow reflective pool was connected to the main swimming pool, spreading across 3,200 square feet and surrounding the living room, kitchen/dining room, hallway, and master bedroom. Keeping the depth at only 15 cm allowed the architects to achieve the desired mirror effect without having to use an excessive amount of water. Underwater steps lead into the deeper area, which reaches approximately 5 feet in depth and runs alongside the living area and terrace. The continuous, glassy appearance of the body of water is facilitated by the 130-foot infinity edge situated along the slope of the lot and a trough inserted between the house and the pool into which the water overflows.

By keeping the water level flush with the main floor, the house seems
to float within the surrounding body of water, creating a sense of
weightlessness and fusion with the natural landscape.

Photos © Geraldine Brunee

## Private Residence

Location: Faqra, Lebanon

Architect: Samir Khairallah & Partners and Vladimir

Djurovic Landscape Architecture

This landscape project represents a concept devoted completely to capturing the remarkable view from the stunning location of this private residence. Situated at an altitude of 6,500 feet, the pool and terrace were designed with the objective of taking this advantage to its maximum potential. The program involved developing a cantilevered swimming pool and sitting area that incorporates a shaded structure and a fireplace. Pure forms and a symmetrical layout lend a bold quality to this pool that seems to spill over onto the landscape.

A delicate landscaping design incorporates patches of grass that thread through the paved areas of the garden. Two fireplaces integrated into the pavement frame the sitting area and pool, emphasizing the minimalist nature of the project through their clean, linear design. A small meditation room was also incorporated into the plan, tucked into the hillside to capture the essence of the view and the disappearing edge of the pool.

The structure that supports the upper level frames the stunning
views of the mirror-like water, which seems to merge with the natural
landscape beyond. The swimming pool was designed to incorporate
a waterfall, which overflows from the upper level in a dramatic sweep
that brings the still body of water to life.

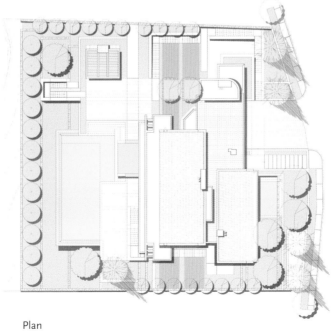

Plan

Photos © Tuca Reinés

# Maravilha Guesthouse

Location: Fernando de Noronha, Brazil

Architect: Bernardes Jacobsen Arquitetura

This guesthouse features a spectacular infinity pool with views over the Atlantic Ocean. It is located on the Brazilian archipelago of Fernando de Noronha, which lies approximately 220 miles from the mainland. The volcanic mountains that protrude from the water generate a striking scenery which this terrace fully takes advantage of through its simple yet stunning design. A wooden terrace with lounge chairs and hammocks wraps around the L-shaped swimming pool that merges with the horizon.

Designed in a tropical yet contemporary style, the shaded terrace was fitted out with chairs that match the wooden deck and face the splendid views of the pool against the ocean. An additional deck exposed to the sky features an arrangement of beds and pillows on which to enjoy the warmth during the day or watch the stars at night time. The elevated position of the pool emphasizes the infinity effect produced by the negative edge of the pool, allowing the pool water and ocean to become one.

The material chosen to line the interior shell of the pool generates a
hue that perfectly matches that of the ocean beyond.

## Yoder Residence

Location: Phoenix, AZ, USA

Architect: Michael P. Johnson

Designed in the spirit of modernist masters such as Wright, Schindler, and Mies van der Rohe, this 5,000-square-foot residence empbodies the characteristics of a modern classic made unique by the particular style of the architect. Anchored to Camelback Mountain on the east, the elegantly simple form soars across the site, supported on the other side by an elevator tower and a sheer wall from which the bedroom cantilevers above the valley floor as the mountain drops away.

The outdoor living space opens to the south, over looking the swimming pool, fire pit, and spa as well as the lush green vegetation that separates the pool fencing and the tile patio. A three-foot-high wall with protruding steel angles contains the patio and pool, which stands out for its negative edge that juts out toward the horizon, emphasizing the stunning views from the house and its relationship with the landscape. Built in Gunite and finished in black Hydrazzo, the pool's edge and waterfall surface were laid with black ceramic tiles.

The roof of the residence extends 16 feet toward the east, providing shade for the outdoor dining area.

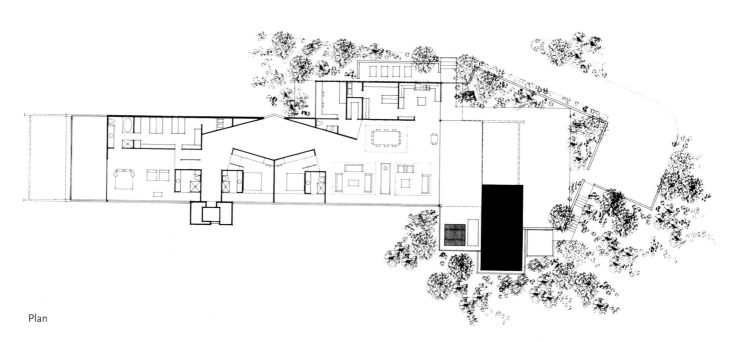

Plan

44

## KM 5 House

Location: Ibiza, Spain

Architect: Bruno Erpicum & Partenaires

Overlooking the town of Ibiza and the Mediterranean Sea, this spectacular residence designed in the style Ibiza's typical white box houses stands out for its privileged location and grand appearance. While the interior spaces of the house are virtually excavated into the mountain, the exterior spaces project outward toward the landscape to engulf the intense white light of the island and its magnificent views.

The terrace is composed of horizontal volumes in the form of long benches from which to contemplate the views, and that also provide shade to the lounge areas. The minimalist, rectangular swimming pool stretches lengthwise across the site, forming a symmetrical composition in which it takes center stage. The portico structure frames this composition and captures the infinity edge of the pool, merging the pool water with the natural landscape that surrounds the building. The white lining of the pool emphasizes the luminosity of the materials and the radiant character of the water against the sky.

Photos © Tuca Reinés

## Tijucopava House

Location: São Paulo, Brazil

Architect: Isay Weinfeld

Set in the town of Tijucopava near São Paulo, this house was designed by the Brazilian architect Isay Weinfeld for the Bitter family, owners of a textile company that produces fabric for some of Brazil's top fashion designers. The 6,500-square-foot beachfront getaway features an over-flowing, rectangular pool set within an elevated terrace that overlooks a narrow, landscaped lawn and the waves that break on the shore.

The house is composed of minimalist white volumes, culminating in a 16-foot-tall living area with towering glass doors that open onto the wooden pool deck. Dark blue mosaic was used to line the basin of the pool, which lends the water a deep blue tone that emulates the color of the ocean and generates vivid reflections of the surrounding trees and constantly changing skyscape. The proximity of the beach is emphasized by the overflowing edge of the pool and the elevated position of the ter-race. A series of wide steps on either side of the structure leads down to the green lawn and sandy beach ahead.

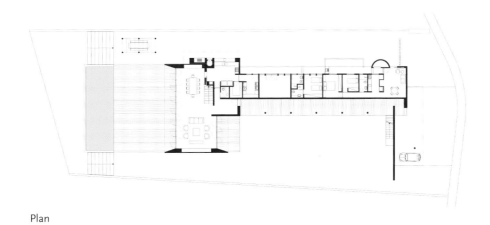

Plan

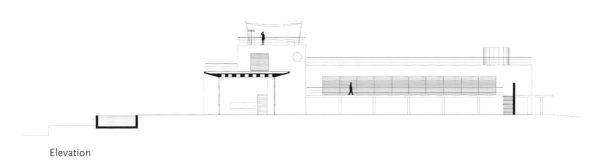

Elevation

Details such as the pebble wall along the side of the pool structure
and the visible grass in between the steps afford this pool
and terrace an original look.

Photos © Tuca Reinés

## House in the Mountains

Location: Rio de Janeiro, Brazil

Architect: Bernardes Jacobsen Arquitetura

Nestled within the mountains not far from Rio de Janeiro, this pool sits atop a hillside with beautiful views of the surrounding serra and lush terrain. The landscaped garden that contains the pool features a series of paved surfaces in different shapes that create an organic pattern in tune with the natural setting. This paved area serves as a transition from house to garden, and in turn leads to the pool entry, which is composed of long steps that run the length of the pool basin.

The mirror-like body of water is modest in size and triangular in shape, adapting to the contour of the hill by means of a curve along the edge of the site. A virtually imperceptible drainage system was installed around the structure to maintain the water at ground level and thus create an infinity effect. Viewed from the house, this illusion is emphasized in such a way that the water receddes into the landscape. The deep blue color results in a highly reflective surface that reproduces the image of the surrounding trees and sky on the water itself.

The subtlety of the design and natural aspect of the pool make for a
genuinly organic appearance that merges with its setting.

## Pacific Heights

Location: Playa Potrero, Costa Rica

Architect: Juan Roca Vallejo and Daniel Coen

In order to take full advantage of the spectacular vantage point provided by the location of this home, the owners and architects opted for a striking pool design with large proportions, organic forms, and an infinity edge nearly 50 feet in length. A specialized structural system was developed to anchor the pool securely between the house, situated at the top of a mountain, and the cliff at the border of the lot.

The swimming pool imitates the forms and materials found in natural bodies of water, such as the asymmetrical curved contour, the granite pebbles used to line the border, and the gray-blue interior chosen to match the color of the Pacific Ocean that lies beyond. A concrete-based molded material simulates natural stone on the terrace, while the pool entry in front of the living area was conceived as a shoreline. The pool encloses slightly more than 1,000 square feet of water at a depth of up to 5 feet. The channel along the outer rim of the pool that collects the overflowing water also serves as a safety barrier between the pool and the cliff.

At night the artificial illumination of the pool mimics the effects of
the sunset along the horizon and reveals the infinity edge of the pool.

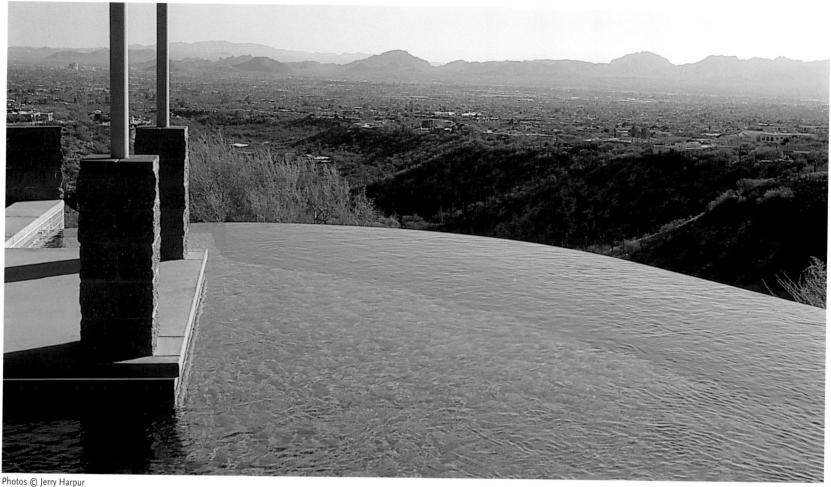

Photos © Jerry Harpur

# Stiteler Residence

Location: Tucson, AZ, USA

Architect: Patio Pools (original pool shell) and Steve

Martino & Associates (landscaping)

This pool in Tucson, Arizona, offers an oasis in the middle of a place known for its extremely dry climate and scorching temperatures. While the original pool shell was built before the current owner bought the property, the terrace and exterior features of the existing structure were added later by landscape architect Steve Martino. The addition included the creation of a deck, a porch structure, and external walls surrounding the pool shell.

The asymmetrical pool follows a vaguely L-shaped form that incorporates an infinity border along its curved outer edge. The structure wraps around the terrace and house so that the Jacuzzi is situated on one side of the residence and the pool entrance is situated next to the shaded terrace at the other end. Its infinity edge is achieved through an angled border composed of mosaic tiles that disappear under the overflowing plane of water. A grayish-blue pool lining gives the water a turquoise hue that matches the sky and, at dusk, reflects the changing colors of the sunset.

Photos © Jordi Miralles

# Tempate

Location: Santa Cruz, Costa Rica

Architect: Juan Roca Vallejo

Designed to resemble a natural oasis, this pool is surrounded by a green, open space that encompasses the large garden belonging to a Mediterranean-style house. Situated approximately 65 feet from the home and taking advantage of the natural slope of the land, the pool opens out in an irregular, circular form and culminates in an infinity edge that looks out over the heavily forested valley.

A gradual descent to the pool mimics the terrain of the seashore and leads into the broad body of water, punctuated by protruding rocks and palm trees. The structure was built with a combination of materials that reflect a gray-blue tone similar to that of natural springs. Enclosing a total surface area of 1,345 square feet, the pool widens to nearly 50 feet-ideal for lap swimming-and also boasts an infinity border that extends about 80 feet on its own. At night, an automated lighting system illuminates the pool from within, creating a dramatic effect against the dark landscape.

The use of organic shapes and the integration of raw materials can
result in a more natural-looking body of water best suited
for houses surrounded by nature.

The entry to the pool is lined with rocks and gradually
sloped to resemble a natural shoreline.

## Residence in Rio

Location: Rio de Janeiro, Brazil

Architect: Bernardes Jacobsen Arquitetura

Boasting a view of Corcovado's Cristo Redentor and the Rio de Janeiro coastline, this pool takes advantage of a modestly sized plot and exclusive location. The neatly landscaped terrace is characterized by its pattern of paved squares outlined by patches of grass, while the pool's intense color was specifically chosen to blend with the turquoise and blue tones of the water near the shore. Given its orientation, only one edge needed to be submerged to produce an infinity effect between the two bodies of water.

The lavish vegetation and abundance of greenery not only enrich the scenic views, but also grant the terrace a great degree of privacy. The interior lining of the pool was meticulously chosen to obtain the glistening and colorful effect achieved by the varying tones of mosaic tiles. As seen here, despite a pool's relatively small size, the implementation of an infinity edge can create the illusion of a larger body of water.

The perspective from within the pool often magnifies the sensation
of abundant water and continuity with the landscape.

## Benioff Pool

Location: St. Helena, CA, USA

Architect: Lundberg Design

This pool and spa sit at the top of a knoll overlooking the Napa Valley and Lake Hennessey. Covering an area of about 100 feet, the expansive body of water adopts a curved shape along the outer edge of the pool. This teardrop edge mimics the form of the knoll and incorporates an infinity edge so that from inside the pool, the water seems to disappear into the valley below. The colors and materials used were chosen for their organic nature and ability to integrate with the surrounding environment.

A hot tub was situated at the pointed end of the curve, creating a continuity that takes advantage of the desired shape of the pool. Indian jade slate was used for the paving and coping stones, while an ipe wood deck was erected on the hillside to provide views over the brimming body of water. In order to protect the existing oak trees on the site, the wall foundations were designed to cantilever over the root system, allowing for an abundance of foliage that emphasizes the insertion of the pool into the edge of the hillside.

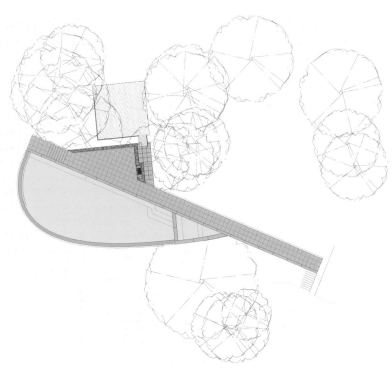

Plan

Photos © Geraldine Bruneel

# Elie Saab Residence

Location: Faqra, Lebanon

Architect: Charles Rizk and Vladimir Djurovic

Landscape Architecture

The plan for this residential chalet was to create a space in which to both savor moments of private contemplation and celebrate memorable gatherings. The client, one of Lebanon's leading international haute couture designers, wished to complement his modern lifestyle, but, more importantly, to create a retreat in which to host special events or simply relax in private.

The lower level represents a strong linear design composed of two simple rectangles: a raised swimming pool and a flat terrace with two integrated recessed sitting areas. The overflowing border of the pool and the angle of view resulting from its elevated position produce a seamless border between the water's surface and the lavish mountain range beyond, achieving an infinity effect that fuses architecture and landscape.

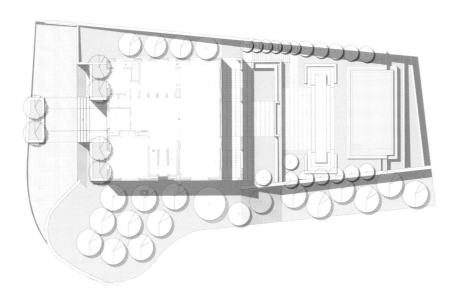

Plan

Viewed from the terrace, the rectangular body of water emphasizes the horizontal nature of the landscape and reflects the stillness and beauty of the natural environment.

Photos © Xavier Mollà

# Residence in Valencia

Location: Valencia, Spain

Architect: Ramon Esteve Estudio de Arquitectura

The irregularity of the terrain on which this house was built inspired the architectural forms that compose the house and garden. Absorbing the slope of the land through a series of stone volumes, the new structure acts as a platform from which to embrace the views over the valley. The architect took advantage of this slope by placing the pool at the boundary of the lot, creating a body of water that disappears over the edge.

The large volumes employed serve as a constant reference to the scale and grandeur of the landscape, while the clean lines and geometric forms contrast with the organic nature of the site. The pool adopts an L-shaped form flanked on the far side by a sunken walkway that leads up to the terrace. A stone wall encircles the structure, forming a channel that collects the overflowing water and generates the infinity effect of the pool.

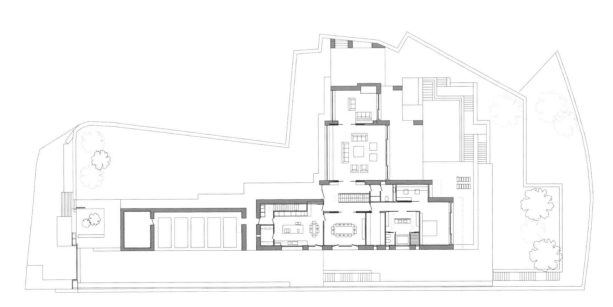

Plan

The interiors of the pool and Jacuzzi were lined with blue mosaic,
while the exterior walls were built with the same stone that
was used for the residential structure.

## Medieval House in Panzano

Location: Florence, Italy

Architect: Marco Pozzoli

Situated within an extensive property that features a medieval house dating back to 1200 that is now home to a family, as well as one of the most important breeding stables for international racehorses, this pool takes on a more rustic design that complements the country-style residence and the rural context in which it is located. The architects took advantage of the site emphasizing the views over the valley by designing an infinity pool that drops off the border of the lot.

The pool assumes an asymmetrical shape that is integrated into the surrounding garden and green landscape. A detailed finish and fine materials, such as stone to line the inner structure and decorate the outer rims, imbue the pool with elegance and distinction. The structure incorporates a small fountain that spills water over a series of steps, creating a cascade effect. This, together with its irregular form, broad dimensions, and infinity edge, lend the pool a natural aspect that allows it to blend in with the rural landscape and make the most of the breathtaking views.

This countryside pool employs natural elements such as stones and
large rocks to generate an elegant design that harmonizes
with its rural surroundings.

# Lundberg Cabin

Location: Sonoma, CA, USA

Architect: Lundberg Design

This pool forms part of a cabin that sits in the midst of 12 acres of redwood trees and overlooks a wooded river canyon towards the northeast, approximately two hours north of San Francisco. Despite its modest surface area of 1,100 square feet, the large deck and open plan make the different areas feel spacious. The project was built mostly with materials reclaimed from various other remodeling projects over the years, integrating objects and materials that had become obsolete and recycling them to perform a new function.

The pool is undoubtedly the most notable example of this practice. Having once served as a water tank for livestock, this 25-foot-wide and 14-foot-deep tub makes for an original swimming pool with an authentic and alternative design. The raised deck integrates the tank structure so that its surface remains flush with the floor, creating a virtually seamless union between the two. Brimming with water, the pool provides an inviting vessel in which to take a dip, especially under a full moon.

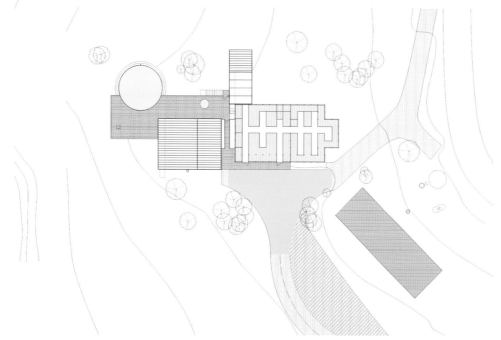

Plan

## Los Sueños

Location: Nosara, Costa Rica

Architect: Juan Roca Vallejo

Integrated into a mountainous landscape, this pool is set within the tropical garden of a house that adopts a mixture of Moroccan and Mediterranean styles. The terrace, made of concrete and covered with natural
stone, incorporates a pergola at the far end of the pool that is built out
of wooden posts. The rectangular pool measures a total of 40 feet long
and 13 feet wide and varies from approximately 4 to 5 feet deep.

Extending toward the west, the pool culminates in a U-shaped infinity
border that overlooks the densely wooded terrain. The pool includes a
square, shallow area with broad steps for entering the water, sitting, or
receiving a relaxing hydro massage. A polished, gold-toned natural stone
from Turkey was used to construct the outer border, while the interior
was lined with turquoise stone from Indonesia. The wooden pergola that
extends across the pool frames the view of the overflowing water against
the tropical landscape and the intense colors of the sunset.

An open-air hut situated on one side of the terrace serves as an exterior
lounge and relaxation area, and features a pool table and hammocks
in which to lie back and enjoy the views from beneath the shade.

The water slips over the edge of the far end of the pool, which is
made out of natural stone slabs.

# Jalan Ampang

Location: Singapore, Singapore

Architect: Guz Architects

In Singapore, land is at a premium because it is scarce. For this reason, many houses are built vertically and often situate gardens and patios on the ground floor, where they are overshadowed by the proximity of the surrounding buildings and the presence of thick vegetation. The designers of this house avoided this drawback by creating a rooftop garden and pool, lifting the exterior spaces toward the sky in order to take full advantage of the light and views.

Situated atop a hill, the raised pool and roof garden not only enjoy cool breezes and spectacular vistas of the landscape, but also allow for additional surface area in the ground floor space. An infinity pool was created to emphasize the feeling of spaciousness and undefined borders. Only one infinity edge was introduced due to the difficulty of maintaining drainage around the entire perimeter of the pool. The pool water disappears over the far end of the basin, offering a breathtaking sensation from within the pool and impressive views from the rooftop terrace.

The submerged edge of the pool was fabricated in glass to heighten
the sense of transparency and create the infinity effect.

Photos © Eugeni Pons

# Pool Garden in Girona

Location: Girona, Spain

Architect: Unknown

This pool garden overlooks the city and mountains from atop Girona's Montjuïc, located on the north side of the old city. Situated on the border of a steep hill, the garden is enclosed by a wooden fence that wraps around the outer perimeter of the site. The infinity pool constitutes the central element of the garden, commanding scenic views of the city and extending outward toward the landscape.

The outdoor space is reminiscent of classical gardens, employing a portico structure that hovers over the pool to frame the views from within the residence. The pool adopts a T-shape that allows for a slight curve on one side and spills over the precipice by way of an infinity edge, offering the illusion of continuity. Behind this edge, the trough that collects the water to be pumped back into the pool remains hidden from sight at all times. The border of the pool, is outlined in wood. A small bridge provides a decorative pathway and a unique place from which to contemplate the scenery.

The wooden border lends this pool a contemporary feel, while the bridge offers the onlooker a unique perspective of the landscape.

## Sydney Harbour

Location: Sydney, Australia

Architect: Luigi Rosselli, Vladimir Sitta (landscape architect)

Originally built in the 1950s and inspired by the work of Frank Lloyd Wright, this waterfront property was renovated by the architect Luigi Rosselli. The house sits on a rock shelf and features a cantilevered balcony that overlooks Sydney Harbour and a new swimming pool that juts out over the rocky shore.

Built above a boat shed and gymnasium situated within the basement of the home, the pool was given a resistant concrete structure to ensure that these spaces remain dry. A concrete bench was placed at the end of the pool nearest the house, while a structural glass wall was introduced to support the water contained within the 50-foot-long shell. This glass wall allows the immersed swimmer to observe the moored boats from beneath the water and virtually merge with the underwater landscape of Sydney Harbor. On the other side of the wall, a tiled trough collects the overflowing water, which is chenneled into a large detention tank and recirculated into the pool.

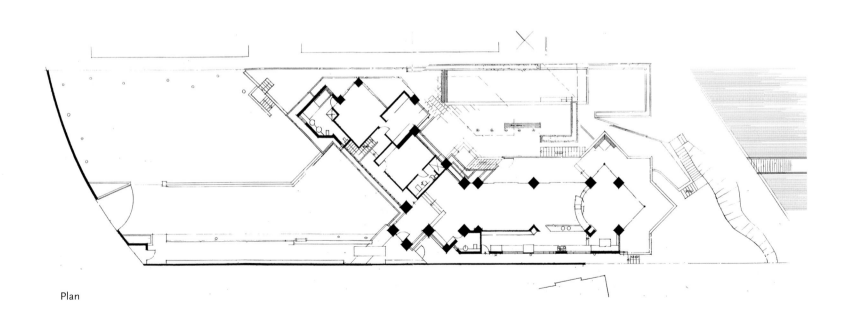

Plan

Photos © Tuca Reinés

# House on the Beach

Location: Recife, Brazil

Architect: Bernardes Jacobsen Arquitetura

Located in northeastern Brazil, this terrace and pool were conceived as a continuation of the stretch of sand and water that surrounds them. The pool adopts a free-form, amoeba-like shape that is partially covered by a porch supported by wooden posts. The tropical character of the design is emphasized by the use of materials and elements indigenous to the region, such as bamboo, wooden logs, and straw.

The pool comprises two environments: a shaded area flanked by a tile-floored terrace and an area exposed to the sun and bordered by a wooden deck. The indefinite shape of the pool and wooden deck mimic the surrounding natural pools and sandbars that form at low tide, in an effort to integrate them with the beachfront setting. Similarly, the color of the pool water is matched to that of the ocean, while the water level is maintained at the same level as the deck to enhance this shoreline effect.

The materials used in this pool terrace-bamboo, wooden logs and
straw-reflect the tropical environment in which it is located.

Photos © Jordi Miralles

# House in Nosara

Location: Nosara, Costa Rica

Architect: Juan Roca Vallejo and Abraham Valenzuela

Situated on a steeply inclined slope, this pool required special attention to construction and a complex structural design to adapt it to its unique location. Distributed over three levels, the house and pool unfold vertically beginning with the upper terrace of the residence, followed by the main access areas, and, on the lowest level, the pool and terrace.

A slight drop in level defines the outer edge of the pool, maintaining the water at nearly the same level as the terrace and eliminating the sense of any defining borders. Emphasizing this borderless effect is the curved infinity edge along the far side of the pool, over which the water seems to disappear onto the steep cliff. The terrace was made out of small riverbed pebbles. A subtle border separates the water from the terrace. A channel along the outer edge of the pool conceals the water-collecting mechanism that enables the infinity edge to function and returns the overflowing water to its original source.

The artificial illumination of the pool set against the darkness of the landscape at night creates the sensation of an abyss at the edge that borders the precipice.

Photos © Eugeni Pons

# House in Fontpineda

Location: Pallejà, Spain

Architect: BPF Arquitectos

This three-story residence features an infinity pool that projects out over the precipice that borders the site. Situated on rather sloping terrain, the 6,500-square-foot house and pool enjoy uninterrupted views of the valley before them. The home consists of three levels: the top level contains the entrance to the residence, the middle level provides access to the garden, and the lower level leads out to the landscaped terrace and pool. The building was situated parallel to the street in order to allocate the maximum amount of area to the exterior spaces.

The south-facing garden and pool adopt a minimalist design that allows the breathtaking views to become the main attribute of the plan. The rectangular pool is framed by a stone tile terrace and a border that disappears along the far edge of the water, which flows over an infinity edge and seemingly drops into the valley. The dark blue color used to line the interior of the pool contrasts intensely with the dominant green shades of the garden and forested areas that surround the house.

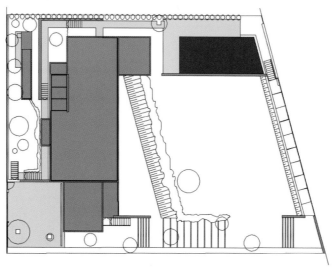

Plan

Photos © Jordi Miralles

# Villa Marrakech

Location: Playa Langosta, Costa Rica

Architect: Juan Roca Vallejo and Abraham Valenzuela

This beachfront pool belongs to a Moroccan-style mansion along the coast of Costa Rica. An elegantly landscaped garden lined with palm trees encloses a T-shaped swimming pool that overlooks the sandy beach located just in front of the property. Situated on an intermediate level between the house and the beach, the pool drops off onto the shoreline, creating an infinity effect as the water seamlessly joins with the landscape beyond.

A grand staircase leads from the mansion down to the pool, which was built out of concrete and structurally designed to adapt to the slope and texture of the terrain. The interior of the pool is lined with a mixture of marble powder, white cement, and dark quartz, reproducing the color of the adjacent ocean. The terrace is covered with small ceramic pieces that have also been used inside the home.

This landscaped garden incorporates an arched gazebo structure
from which to gaze at the elongated body of water. The gazebo offers
an intimate and romantic space for special parties and gatherings.

From the garden, the infinity edge appears as the line at which the pool seems to merge with the beach landscape beyond.

The grand stairway that leads down to the pool accommodates a
long sofa designed to seat a large number of people and allow
panoramic views of the pool and beach.

# Residence on the Coast

Location: Angra dos Reis, Brazil

Architect: Bernardes Jacobsen Arquitetura

Located southwest of Rio de Janeiro, this residence in Angra dos Reis is surrounded by lush tropical vegetation through which it looks onto the ocean shore. The house features an extensive terrace with different functional spaces and shaded areas. Adopting a curved shape on the terrace side, the pool culminates in a straight infinity edge over which the water spills into a designated channel that recycles it back into the pool.

Becaise of the elevated position of the pool structure, this channel remains out of direct sight and is integrated within a landscaped garden on the other side of the pool that occupies its entire length. The slight slope of the terrace into the water eliminates the need for a marked border, emphasizing the expansive character of the pool. White mosaic tiles line the interior of the pool shell, producing a luminous blue tone that reflects the white residential structure and the limestone terrace that envelops it.

The view from the terrace captures the infinity effect produced by the
submerged edge of the pool.

Photos © Pep Escoda

# House on the Sea

Location: Murcia, Spain

Architect: Estudio Muher

This project consists of a single-family house built on a cliff overlooking the sea along the southwestern coast of Spain. Conceived as a boat, the residence is accessed through the top floor via a walkway that cantilevers over the garden and proceeds through the upper terrace that overlooks the pool and also provides shade to the outdoor lounge area underneath. In this way, the architects managed to provide a continuous view of the sea from virtually every point inside the home.

Given the difficulties presented by the craggy terrain on which the structure is situated, the house was developed as a series of overlapping levels and platforms, providing parking spaces, a landscaped terrace, and an infinity pool that spills over into the scenic backdrop. The pool's curved shape makes room for tall palm trees, plants, and large boulders taken from the site itself. The incorporation of vegetation adds color and contrast to the monochromatic and arid landscape, while the rocks and the stones embrace elements typical of this area of the coast.

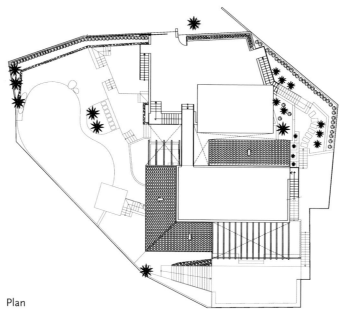

Plan

# Brosmith House

Location: Beverly Hills, CA, USA

Architect: SPF Architects

This single-family residential project is sensitively sited on a ridgeline of the Mulholland Scenic Parkway, overlooking the San Fernando Valley in southern California. In keeping with the client's objectives, the structure projects the exterior space as living space and harnesses the panoramic views of the valley below, which are accessible from the common areas and courtyards of the property. Separate living pods along the central spine of the house allow different activities and interactions to occur simultaneously without mutual disruption.

The pool juts out toward the commanding view and is partially surrounded by the concrete terrace. The overflowing water on the far side and the lateral border produce a strong visual impact, especially from within the pool. Its simple, rectangular form follows the modern, linear aspect of the house structure and focuses greater attention on the interaction between the architecture and the landscape, rather than on the design itself.

The pool structure employs a system that permits the water to flow
over the edge, creating the infinity effect. Full-length glass panels
reveal a panorama of the surrounding terrace, allowing
the tenants to take advantage of the stunning views
of the pool against the San Fernando Valley.

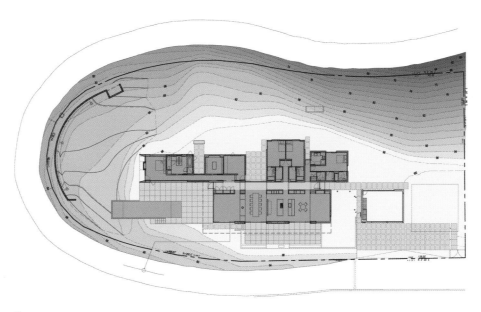

Plan

# Westcliff Estate

Location: Johannesburg, South Africa

Architect: Studio Mas

Inspired by the residential work of legendary architects like Frank Lloyd Wright and Le Corbusier, the design of this house emphasizes the concept of horizontality as a way of paying homage to the landscape. The far-reaching infinity pool serves as the transitional element between the house and the man-made landscape of Johannesburg and Magaliesburg beyond.

Situated on a sloping hillside, the cantilevered pool is supported from underneath by a series of stout, mushroom-shaped concrete columns, which can be seen upon arriving at the site. From inside the residence, the main focus become the pool, which is framed by a large terrace that runs its length and provides panoramic views of the horizon. A drain on either side of the pool collects the overflowing water to create the infinity effect, generating a view that blurs the boundary between the body of water and the natural surroundings. The pool was lined with materials in a dark tone to simulate the appearance of a natural lake or pond.

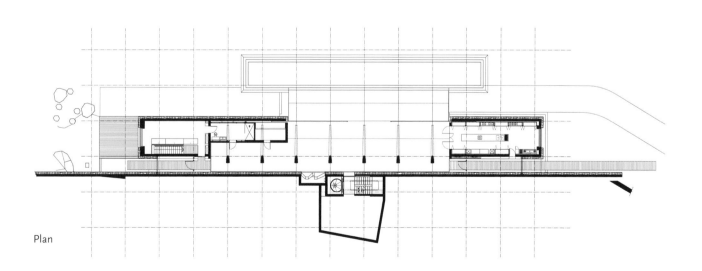

Plan

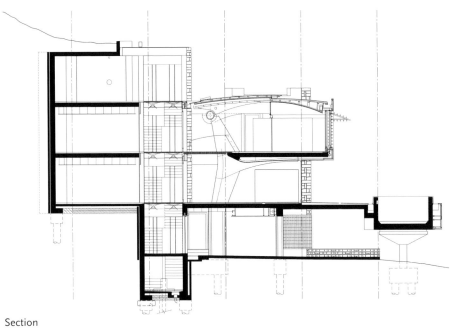

Section

The living room, terrace, and swimming pool were situated on the
same plane to maximize the expansive views, converting the
landscape into the main element of the design.

Photos © Geraldine Bruneel

## Bassil Residence

Location: Faqra, Lebanon

Architect: Kamal Homsi and Vladimir Djurovic

Landscape Architecture

Conceived as a vacation chalet for short visits throughout the year, this residence was designed to accommodate guests and host lively gatherings and special events. The architects were challenged with the task of creating various environments within an extremely narrow site that would cater to different kinds of activities. They achieved by emplyoing a series of illusions and careful manipulations to yield the maximum sense of space and enhance the experience.

The plan consists of various sitting areas, a cantilevered Jacuzzi, a covered bar, a swimming pool, and a large entertainment terrace with bench, fireplace, and barbeque. The shaded sitting area and negative-edge swimming pool frame the breathtaking views of the surrounding mountain ranges, while floating steps made of solid stone and red cedarwood afford the onlooker a unique perspective of the landscape from within the pool itself, further enhancing the visual experience obtained from such a high altitude.

The base of this raised water mirror is covered with black river-washed pebbles, which are visible when the sunlight hits the water.

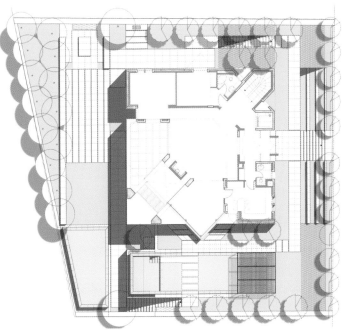

Plan

One of the stone steps extends out over the pool, providing access to
the cantilevered Jacuzzi situated at the very edge of the site.

# Directory

Barry Beer Design
10539 Clarkson Road
Los Angeles, CA 90064, USA
Tel.: +1 310 204 6228
Fax: +1 310 204 6220
www.barrybeerdesign.com

Bernardes Jacobsen Arquitetura
Rua Corcovado 250
22460-050 Rio de Janeiro, Brazil
Tel./Fax: +55 11 3082 6834
www.bja.com.br

BPF Arquitectos
Pau Claris 173, 2° 1ª
08037 Barcelona, Spain
Tel.: +34 934 879 341
Fax: +34 934 879 342

Bruno Erpicum & Partenaires
Avenue Reine Astrid 452
B-1950 Kraainem, Belgium
Tel.: +32 2 687 27 17
Fax: +32 2 687 56 80
www.erpicum.org

Delugan Meissl Associated Architects
Mittersteig 13/4
A-1040 Vienna, Austria
Tel.: +43 1 585 36 90
Fax: +43 1 585 36 90 11
www.deluganmeissl.at

Estudio Muher
Huerto Las Palmeras s/n
30850 Murcia, Spain
Tel.: +34 968 424 682
www.muher.com

Guz Architects
3 Jalan Kelabu
278199, Singapore
Tel.: +65 6476 6110
Fax: +65 6476 1229
www.guzarchitects.com

Isay Weinfeld
Rua Andre Fernandes 175
04536-020 Itaim-Bibi
São Paulo, Brazil
Tel.: +55 11 3079 7581
Fax: +55 11 3079 5656
www.isayweinfeld.com

Juan Roca Vallejo
Aquart, Apartado 35
5200 Nicoya, Costa Rica
Tel./Fax: +1 506 675 0537
www.aquart.net

Luigi Rosselli
15 Randle Street, Surry Hills
Sydney, NSW, Australia 2010
Tel.: +61 2 9281 1498
Fax: +61 2 9281 0196
www.luigirosselli.com

Lundberg Design
2620 Third Street
San Francisco, CA 94107, USA
Tel.: +1 415 695 0110
Fax: +1 415 695 0379
www.lundbergdesign.com

Michael P. Johnson Design Studio
PO BOX 4058
Cave Creek, AZ 85327, USA
Tel.: +1 480 488 2691
Fax: +1 480 488 1656
www.mpjstudio.com

Ramon Esteve Estudio de Arquitectura
Jorge Juan 8, 5° 11ª
46004 Valencia, Spain
Tel.: +34 963 510 434
Fax: +34 963 510 469
www.ramonesteve.com

SPF Architects
8609 East Washington Boulevard
Culver City, CA 90232, USA
Tel.: +1 310 558 0902
Fax: +1 310 558 0904
www.spfa.com

Steve Martino & Associates
111 East Dunlap Avenue, Suite 1-625
Phoenix, AZ 85020, USA
Tel.: +1 602 957 6150
Fax: +1 602 224 5288
www.stevemartino.net

Studio Mas
25 Oxford Road, Forest Town
2132 Johannesburg, South Africa
Tel.: +27 11 486 2979
Fax: +27 11 646 5399
www.studiomas.co.za

Studio Pozzoli
Via delle Cascine 31R
50122 Florence, Italy
Tel.: +39 055 24 66 753

Vladimir Djurovic Landscape Architecture
Rizk Plaza
Broumana, Lebanon
Tel.: +961 4 862 444
Fax: +961 4 862 462
www.vladimirdjurovic.com

Vladimir Sitta/Terragram Pty. Ltd.
3rd Floor, 15 Randle Street
Sydney, NSW, Australia 2010
Tel.: +61 2 9211 6060
Fax: +61 2 9211 6057